I0704288

ETHNOYST MAGAZINE

A Style Guide for Urban Women

Dr. Manika Singla

www.ethnicoyster.com

Overview

Ethnoyst Magazine is designed for anyone who wants to know the secrets to always looking stylish with minimal effort. Especially for today's urban women who have less time to get ready for the office or attend any occasion due to their busy schedules. So here, we not only showcase the latest fashion updates, beauty, styling, grooming, healthy lifestyle tips & DIY ideas to follow but also talk about women's real-life journey and their creative talents.

Furthermore, we also aim to provide a unique platform especially for women in the form of poems, quotations, inspirational stories, infographics, amazing facts, painting images to showcase their creativity in our magazine.

So, read on to find the latest updates of the fashion world, styling advice, shopping tips, DIY ideas, beauty hacks, best health secrets, and relationship advice, all in one place.

Keywords

woman personal style lookbook, top women magazine India, best personal style guide, 2021 dressing trends, ethnic fusion fashion inspiration, female health relationship secrets

Ethnoyst Magazine

Copyright © 2021 by Dr Manika Singla.

For information, contact - Dr. Manika Singla ethnicoyster@gmail.com **(FB | Insta | @ethnoystmagz)**

Website: https://www.ethnicoyster.com

Edition: Vol. 1, February 2021

Preface

In the book, the author distills her secrets into a fun, comprehensive style guide focused on rethinking your wardrobe like a fashion expert and making what's in your closet work for you. She provides real-world advice about everything style-related, including:

- Styling every garment you own in the best way
- Mastering the closet organization
- Which alterations are worth it
- Shopping thrift and vintage like a rockstar

Instead of repeating boring style rules, the author tells us to break the rules and get real about everything from apparel to accessories to showcase inevitable fashion statements. The book has lots of insider tips from the author's arsenal of hacks and expertise.

The author has been a management expert, fashion designer, and writer. She is currently running a design studio named Ethnic Oyster from last 2014. Apart from this, she runs her online profiles on all major social media platforms (Facebook, Instagram, and youtube) by the name of ethnoyst magz and ethnic oyster.

Before this fashion writing and successfully running this clothing venture, she worked as a professor and researcher in the management domain for many years. Several research papers, books, and articles in diverse domains of management, tourism, and fashion are published for known national, international journals and related sites.

Flair for writing, passion for designing the fabrics as well as self-learning about the technical aspects of the digital world had encouraged her to enter into this stream. Utilizing her previous skills of writing as a blogger and learning by doing through exhibitions & networking gives her the direction to move ahead progressively.

Introduction

Ethnoyst Magazine: A Style Guide for Urban Women

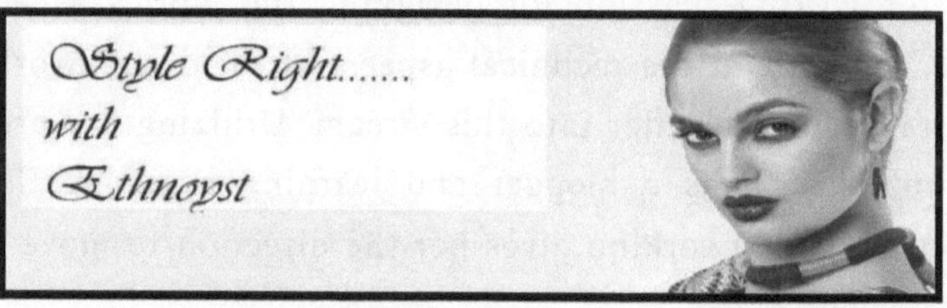

Ethnoyst Magazine is designed for all those who want to dress better and improve their style. The book will help you to determine your body shape and guide you through the step-by-step process on how to dress according to your body shape and size to enhance your assets and draw attention away from problem areas.

This book will show you how to create your capsule wardrobe with key pieces and explains to you how to mix and match items to create a variety of outfits. It is filled with several styling tips, beauty hacks, and health & relationship secrets along with trends to make the most with the accessories to achieve an effortless glamour and style quotient.

A must-read especially for the urban women who want to look fabulous and confident with minimal effort. The magazine not only uncovers the real journey and other talents of the inspiring women but also the new fashion terms for the style casters.

Read on to find the latest fashion news, get the styling advice, shopping tips, DIY ideas, and fashion know-how, all in one place.

To conclude, Style is both complex and simple. It is about striking a balance and mastering it!

Table of Contents

Chapter 1

Five fashion trends to follow in the year 2021

Tags: 2021 fashion trends, five fashion trends, florals, garages, indo-westerns, monotone fashion, short k Kurti suits.

Five fashion trends to follow in the year 2021

Here are the five fashion trends to be followed this year.......

1. There is a shift from long Kurti to short Kurtis this year. Short Kurtis can be worn with dhoti pants, salwar, skirts, or any type of bottom wear. Only length alteration type ended, the rest of the style is colors.

2. Garara suits either in plain/embroidered are in this year. Celebrities were spotted with Shararas last year. In comparison to Sharara Suits of the past, this season, it's the year of Gararas !!

3. Indian fabrics with westerns silhouettes is another major trend that is going to be seen this summer. Such as Kantha work jackets, jorjat maxi chikankari dresses. You may design your jackets, tunics & blazers using Indian fabrics and be seen as trendy and fashionable as you are.

4. Monotone fashion from head to toe be it a dress, footwear or jewelry is the new upcoming trend. Monotone dresses instead of contrasting colors of last year will be the next fashion statement. Accordingly, it's the elegant year of monotones. Then there are floral printed outfits from last year that will be noticed this year too.

5. Sabyasachi lehengas and Satya Paul sarees were seen with floral prints last season. You can flaunt your drapes, lehengas, sarees, suits in florals on your special days effortlessly.

5 Simple Rules for a Happy Life

1. Don't be ~~overly emotional.~~

=Have faith.

2. Don't ~~ever give up.~~

=Keep Trying.

3. Don't make things ~~complicated.~~

=Keep it Simple.

4. Don't take things ~~too seriously.~~

=Laugh at Problems.

5. Don't be a ~~grown-up.~~

=Stay as youthful as a kid.

Chapter 2

Confused about how to wear prints?

Tags: colors, mix, and match, prints, prints combination, prints combination tips, types of prints

Confused about how to wear prints?

So we are giving you here, 10 very simple and easy tricks on how to have a mix and match prints combination:

1. Firstly, the base color should be the same. It could be dotted, florals or stripes. The color uniformity should be there for instance if there is black then it should be all black, green then it should be all green

2. In case you are not getting the same color prints, they should be from the same family colors for example black and blue, red and orange tones, or more. So, use single-family colors!!

3. If you are not getting the same color or same family color prints, then match prints with solid color r eg. Contrasting colors create balance as there is no risk for a combination.

4. Prints placed differently – If you want to wear the overall same print, then don't wear the same print for an attire, however, you can use the same print placed differently e dots placement should be far on top and dots nearby on the bottom.

5. Same Pattern in Different Sizes– Use variations in size such as use dots, stripes, or floral pattern in large sizes for the Bottom and small size for top

6. Use Inverted Colours for instance if the shirts are black-white as the top then use white black are bottom, or make use of different base colors and paint colors a

7. Using **Bright & Neutral Colours** Combination is another best idea to balance for multi printed garments.

8. STRIPES - Stripes are the new neutral. Use graphic lines as a base for bottoms and tops

9. BLOCK IT - Do mix contrasting prints If the prominent shades within them are from the same color family. Get the trend from head to heels for the maximalist to work it. Keep silhouettes ladylike for a chic finish.

10. MATCH POINT - Go matchy! Skirts and tops decorated with the same patterns different colorways playfully chic for the day.

Plaids

Scales

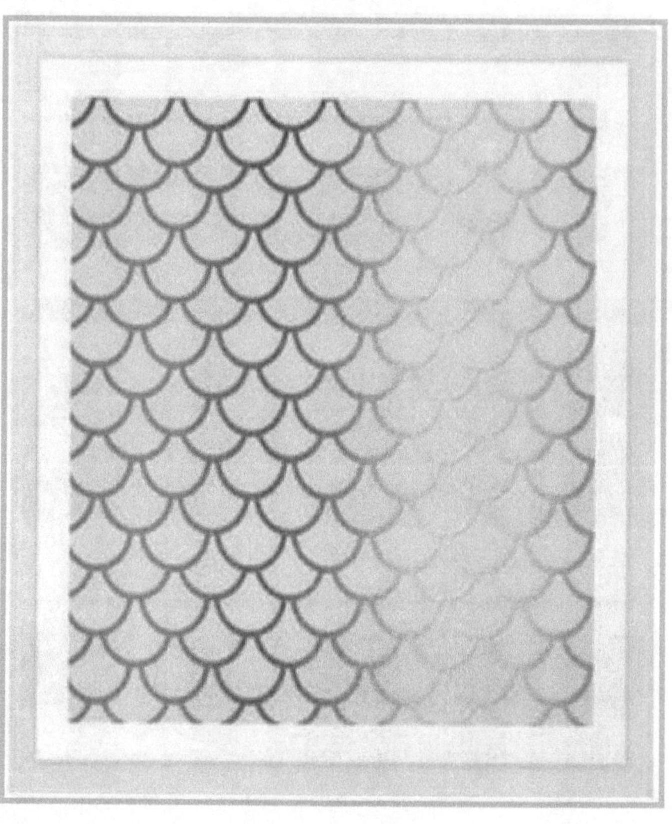

Damask

Chevron

Honeycomb

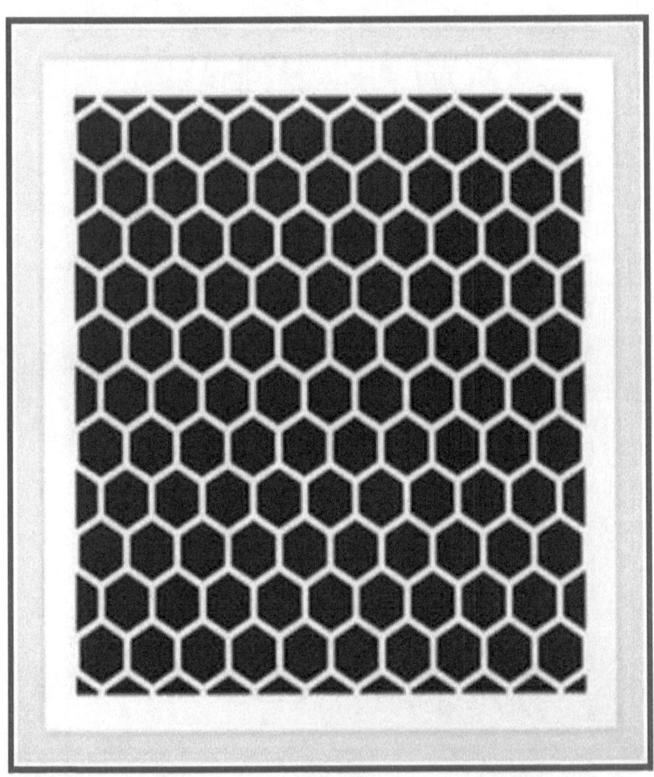

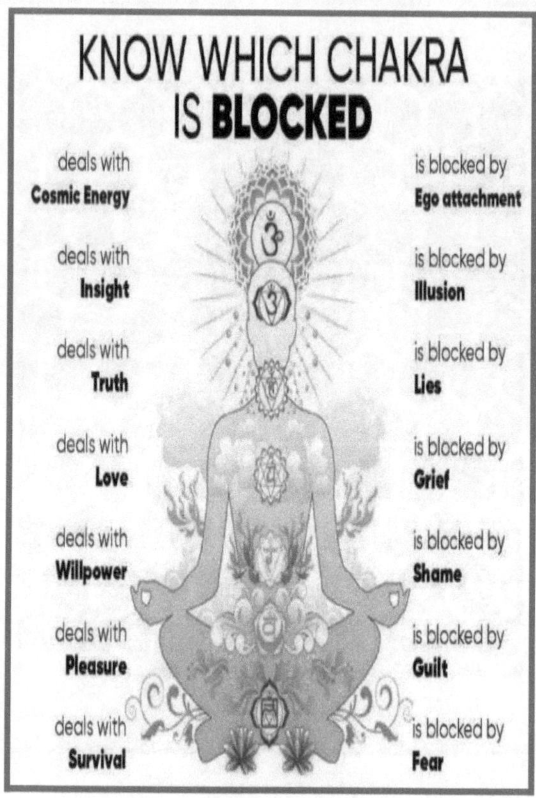

KNOW WHICH CHAKRA
IS BLOCKED
deals with
Cosmic Energy
is blocked by
Ego attachment
deals with
Insight
is blocked by
Illusion
deals with
Truth
is blocked by
Lies
deals with
Love
is blocked by
Grief
deals with
Willpower
is blocked by
Shame
deals with
Pleasure
is blocked by
Guilt
deals with
Survival
is blocked by
Fear

Chapter 3

Indian Outfit Ideas for Curvy Women

Tags: Curvy Women, Indian Outfit Ideas for Curvy Women, Indian wear, styling tips

Indian Outfit Ideas for Curvy Women

If you are curvy and like to wear Indian clothing, then there are the following 5 styling tips inspired by Bollywood:

1. Layered Voluminous Bottoms –

You can pair tulip pants, dhoti pants, or harem pants with croKurtisBollywoodth a shrug

2. *Long Flared Jackets –*

Long flared jackets can be paired with Anarkalis and pants. There are different types of jackets like a front slit, side slit, and calendar jackets which can transform the complete outfit. Assemble them with Anarkali, lehenga, or with saree and wear them all year round

3. *Flary Bottoms & Short Kurtis –*

Wear shararas, garages, or skirts as a flared bottom with short kurtis which is an upcoming trend these days.

4. *Broad Necklines –*

You can flaunt your Anarkali or saree blouse with a broad
neckline to have a stunning look

6. *Comfortable fit light/pastel-colored dress with minimal makeup*

This look will surely suit the curvy women on any day occasion

"Fashions fade,
style is eternal."
—Yves Saint Laurent

Chapter 4

Dress Up According To Age

Tags: accessories, age groups, colors, fabrics, necklines, Outfit Ideas, silhouettes, style

Dress Up According To Age

Here, We discuss what suits you as per your age. That is we have segregated the outfit ideas according to your age.

For 50's – Elegance

One should focus on one thing, keeping the other things subtle and tone down. For instance, color, style, or fabric. If you want to give attention to the color element of your dress then you need to keep the other things very simple in terms of style and minimal jewelry.

The name given to fifty-plus age groups is elegance which is aptly defined if you focus on one thing. Similarly, if you want to wear heavily embroidered fabric, then keep the color and style subtle and look down. Again if you go for layered or high-low style, then keep other things less attention-grabbing.

Yes, a straight-line silhouette works the best for you but you can also go for Anarkalis which also looks elegant on you! The fabric must be drapy that should be straight fit and never go for a flouncy one that is fitted to the waist. Soft silk, net, and georgettes suit you the most, So opt for these. Also always focus on one accessory either a large size neckpiece or oversized earrings that attracts attention. There shouldn't be any overloaded look.

40's – Classy

Forty's age group is defined as classy. So to give that classic appearance, you can add collars or go for basic broad necklines. Style of layering that is jacket /shrug for kurta, gown, or dress is an idea for you. Always go for a comfortable fit and say no to any body-hugging outfit.

Shoulder pads in coats or waists will also look good on you giving you a plain sharp look. An important accessory that makes you sophisticated and refined is wearing a watch. Yes, you get a perfect look with one accessory at a time while toning down the other ones!

30's – Glamorous & Feminine

The Indian outfit for the 30's age group is sarees if you don't want to go for a western outfit. In this, your body is properly defined. Fabrics in georgettes or net with curvy sweetheart necklines work the best for you. You can try adding more than one element but that should be balanced. To have a glamorous feminine look, experiment with the silhouettes and opt for multiple-size jewelry along with the dark deep makeup as per the occasion.

20's – Playful

The 20 's age group can try outfit ideas of any age group be it 30s, 40s, or 50s. Being playful, they can follow any age group. The bright colors will suit them the most.

They can mix and match and hence there are no restrictions. Everything works out for them, be it a salwar suit, an A-line kurta, or a straight kurta set. They can opt for draped pants or carry a ruffled style saree and pair them up with any type of accessories. Even an ageless saree that is a silk saree is ideal for them. Besides, All colors suit them. But, the white or ivory color with a hint of gold or gold detailing work would be most apt for them.

Here, we just gave you directions to follow however there are no restrictions to age as such. Because at the end of the day, instead of outfit your vibrant personality matters!!

IT'S ABOUT WHO STAYS
NOT WHO PROMISED

Chapter 5

Personalized Valentine's Day Gifts

Tags: valentine's day gifts for her, valentines gifts

Personalized Valentine's Day Gifts:

Love is divine and that is there on; one needs to accept that the blossom of the feeling of love for each other happens due to the grace of the Almighty Lord. This spiritual thought needs to be added with some creatively crafted Valentine Gift to make the lover feel blushed on the very special day.

The online gifts shopping portal, Giftcart.com brings the tremendous treasure of the most fascinating love gift ideas that would be designed to bring a smile to the partner's face and make the occasion truly memorable.

It would be a special feeling to receive something carrying my name or image printed on it. Such gifts would multiply the joy of receiving the gift.

Here are a few marvelous gift ideas online specially designed for V day:

Personalized Mixed Photos Puzzle

Valentine's Day would be the special opportunity to impress the partner by expressing love most creatively. This jigsaw puzzle frame can be among the most innovatively designed valentine's day gifts as it carries multiple couple images compiling the most memorable moments to last for years ahead. This frame can be kept in the showcase or anywhere in the living room, bedroom, or even on the working desk in the office as well.

Personalized Picture Clock

The romantic snaps taken during the trips or captured casually can be compiled to be printed on the wall clock. Giftcart.com helps to bring the sweetest memories on the clock that would surely add a smile to the receiving partner's face. The creative idea would remain next to the eyes of the partners as the lock would be retained for years ahead on any wall at home.

Mug with A Twist

Valentine's Day can be the best opportunity to encourage the partner to celebrate. Eventually, favorite c led beer can be the perfect mode to add spice to the celebration. This beer mug with a meaningful message including the name of the receiving partner engraved on it could be one of the trickiest Valentine 's Day presents that help to express the innermost emotions of love.

10 Inch I Love You Brown, Personalised Teddy

Soft toys, especially teddy bears, play a very interesting role in conveying emotions from soul to soul. This 10 inch furry, brown teddy is made to look additional due to the t-shirt it wears carrying the love message and the names of the couple celebrating V Day.

Personalized Love Story Cushion

The soft cushion has the photograph of the couple printed on it along with the text message that calls their love story the 'favorite'. This cushion can be kept on the sofa, any chair, or even on the bed to remember the special occasion and feel the warmth of the love of the partner through many years ahead. The cushion would create a wonderful gesture that keeps the coupe emotionally united.

Postcard Message Bottle

We are enjoying the privileges of the fastest communication in the digital era today. However, the beauty and the desperate feeling to open the love letter from the beloved remains the same. This gift puts the sweet and short love letter into a glass bottle with a vase and adds it to an eye-catching postcard. As this postcard is delivered to the doorstep or presented personally on the very special Valentine's Day; the receiving partner of any age group would fall in love again for sure.

Giftcart is a wonderful place online to get the most surprising and interesting love gifts that are most appropriate to gift the loving partner on Valentine's Day. Apart from this special occasion, Giftcart has a collection of best-suited gift ideas for various occasions and expressions.

"People say that you're going the
wrong way when it's simply a way
of your own."

ANGELINA JOLIE

Chapter 6

12 Tips to make your hair look beautiful

Tags: hair care, hair care tips

12 Tips to make your hair look beautiful

If you dream of a perfect hairstyle and perfect hair, forget about expensive salon treatments for hair in salons. They would rather empty your wallet than cure your hair. Instead, add 12 good habits to your daily hair care, which will help improve your appearance and health. I collected advice from the best stylists and hairdressers on how to care for hair at home. All this is easy to do from the comfort of your own home.

Avoid high temperatures

Of course, sometimes using a hairdryer or ironing is inevitable,
but try to minimize the use of a hairdryer, ironing, or curling.
Which will ensure the smoothness of the hair for six months?
If you want curls, try the good old hair curlers and let your hair dry naturally. By letting your hair rest one or two days a week, you will get healthier and more vibrant hair in the future.
If you need to use a hairdryer and a curler, do not forget about thermal protection for the hair, as well as the choice of devices for styling with the latest technologies (ionization, ceramic, or Teflon coating).

Sleep On A Silk Pillowcase

The smooth texture of the silk covers the cuticles of the hair, and you get up in the morning with smooth, even hair (a cotton pillowcase works the other way around). The satin fabric prevents hair from crushing and creasing, and you can get rid of morning confusion and dryness.

Take Care Of Clean Hair

Perhaps you have heard of a new trend, which is to not use shampoo when washing hair to preserve their natural structure and health. Despite this, most stylists recommend using shampoos in hair care. If you use quality products, washing your hair with shampoo will bring only benefits. Surprisingly, a good shampoo can prevent the cross-section of the ends of the hair, provides the necessary level of moisture, and gives the hair shine and lightness.

Not sure how often you should wash your hair? Take this principle as a basis: if you live in a large, industrial city or walk on the street – wash your hair every day. If you live in a small town, away from industrial facilities, washing every 2-3 days will be enough. But, if the hair is dry at the tips and oily at the roots, you will have to do it every day.

Use Air Conditioning

The scalp needs to be moisturized just like the face, especially if you are currently letting go of your hair. The general rule – be sure to apply a conditioner that suits your hair type every time you wash your hair.

Be A Supporter Of One Brand Of Cosmetics

There is an erroneous opinion that hair can get used to the ingredients of cosmetic products and for them a periodic change of care is useful.
Experts strongly disprove this myth. Instead, it is much more correct to find the perfect product for your hair and be faithful to it all the time. Changing hair care in search of your product is normal, but once you find your best, you should only buy it.

If you are trying to properly care for your hair, using only makeup cosmetics and external methods of exposure, you should know that you are doing only half of the work. To achieve success, it is important not only to look outside but also from the inside. Try these latest hairstyles for girls to flaunt every day.
What we eat plays a huge role in the speed of hair growth and its quality. A diet rich in iron, zinc, omega-3 fatty acids, and protein helps to stimulate hair follicles and accelerate hair growth.
Nutritionists recommend eating lean red meat, chicken, and fish several times a week to maintain the health of your hair.

Fill Hair With Vitamins

Even if your nutrition is impeccable, you may lack the key vitamins that strengthen the hair. Not sure if your hair needs vitamins?

If there are burrs near your nails, or the skin near them is dry and scaly, then consider it a cry of SOS from your body. Do not worry, it is easy to fix: if you start taking vitamin complexes, minerals, and amino acids, you can get healthy and strong hair as a result of several months of intake. Bonus, this will benefit not only the hair but also the skin and nails.

Limit Sun Exposure To Hair

You know, what damage to your skin can bring in the sun during the day without sunscreen? Did you know that hair suffers as much, if not more? Care for your hair in the sun is also necessary, as well as for the body.

To prevent hair damage from the sun, it is advisable to use a hair conditioner and moisturizer that does not require rinsing every day.

And if you go to the beach, use special sprays for hair in SPF, such can be found in cosmetics stores.

Brush Correctly

Before you comb your hair, be sure to know what you are doing. Take a comb with sparse teeth for particularly tangled hair and always brush them up to avoid tangling

Trim Tips Regularly, Even If You Let Go Of Hair

To grow long hair, we sometimes miss a couple of visits to the hairdresser, but this gives the opposite effect. Experts agree that hair should be cut every 6-8 weeks. This prevents delamination and cross-section of hair.

Wash your head with cool water

Do not use too hot water to wash your hair. Excessive heat can reduce hair volume. Choose warm water when soaping your hair. This allows you to get the required amount of foam to clean the hair. Wash off the shampoo with warm water.
And when it comes to an air conditioner or hair mask, turn on cool water to wash your hair. Coldwater seals nutrients in the hair and gives them a beautiful healthy glow.

Do not overdo the number of cosmetic products

If you cover your entire head with shampoo or conditioner, this is wrong. Care for your hair properly. Use shampoo only on the hair roots, where they are the oiliest and have accumulated the most styling products. On the other hand, the conditioner, on the contrary, should be applied from the middle of the length of the hair down to the tips, which are most prone to dehydration and section.

Use tips on how to care for your hair at home and your hair will be healthy and beautiful without salon procedures and with a minimum of cash investments.

You are precious
and deserving of
the same
kindness and
care you so freely
give to others.
Treat yourself as
the precious
soul you are.
Manika Singla
ETHNOYST MAGAZINE

Chapter 7

How to choose summer jewelry according to your personality?

Tags: accessories, accessory, artificial jewelry, fashion statement, Jewellery Ideas, jewelry trends, jewelry variations, jewelry, lifestyle

How to choose summer jewelry according to your personality?

As we all know, it has become a trend to use special jewels, on different occasions. Now men also have started to wear jewelry in the form of watches, rings, and bracelets. One thing that should be kept in mind that your jewelry should be relevant to your dressing and especially jewels to your skin tone.

But here the question is, how to choose summer jewelry according to personality? In this topic we will explore the most common types of jewelry you can use in summer.

It is a common thing that, in summer when the days get warmer and longer the jewelry you use gets hotter. Summer days are full of sunshine and heat.

Therefore always choose summer jewelry according to your skin tone. Before summer, update your wardrobe, fashion, and jewelry style. Don't try to use metals and gemstones which get hotter in summer. By understanding how different metals affect your skin in summer, you will be able to find a good collection of jewelry for summer.

Focus on your skin tone

It is a common thing, everybody in this world has a different skin tone. So, if you are a jewelry lover, it is very important to determine your skin tone, if you are looking for summer jewelry. Yes, it is necessary because they do not focus on your skin tone, jewelry you wear may damage your skin. So first of all, determine your skin color and tone in natural light and then select suitable jewelry.

Choose bright colors

As we all know, summer is the season with bright sun, blue water and also filled with the beach. Everyone wants to enjoy themselves on the beach in the summer season. So, with all of this fun and color, your jewelry should also have a stylish look according to the summer season. Try to choose the brightest color jewelry and match it with your beachwear to complete your personality.

You can visit a nearby jewelry market to find summer jewelry according to your skin tone. Jewelers use different jewelry display cases and jewelry ring display cases to create a better display. You can choose bright and bold colors according to your style and personality. Choose gems and stones with fun colors to represent your summer jewelry in a cool way.

A nice collection of gems

If you have gems in your collection of jewelry, summer is a really good time to use those gems. You can use your collection of gems on different occasions like a marriage or a birthday party. Furthermore, you can use gems when you are going out with friends for a long walk. The shining of gems in the night will increase the value of your jewelry.

Use bracelets

Bracelet is a piece of jewelry, which is mostly used among women as well as men all over the world. The use of bracelets is increasing day by day and gaining more popularity. It is a piece of jewelry, you can wear at any time of the day.

You can find a collection of bracelets by visiting a jewelry store. After using your good collection of bracelets and other jewelry you can save it by using special portable jewelry display cases for further use. So, it is a good idea to use bracelets in your summer jewelry collection.

Bottom line

When we talk about jewelry, there are no specific rules about metals and jewelry. But still, it is good practice to determine skin tone to avoid any kind of skin damage. If we talk about summer jewelry, bright colors jewelry is the best choice for summer.

Summer is a season for excitement and enjoying the beach with friends. So, always choose summer jewelry according to your age, skin tone, and which correlates with the sunshine and beauty of the summer season.

Fashion
says
"me too"
style says
"only me."
Manika Singla | Ethnoyst Magazine

Chapter 8

How to Look Slimmer Instantly

Tags: wardrobe weapon, suitable hairstyle, makeup tricks, black dress, body posture, heels, monotone color

How to Look Slimmer Instantly

If you hate counting calories or watching your weight every second day, we understand that!

That is exactly why we are here to help you with some simple and stylish tricks to stop looking bigger and start looking better!

Here are some wardrobe, fashion, makeup, and styling rules that will make you look slimmer instantly. So, read on to take a few tips.

Wardrobe Weapon

The perfect bodies that you see on television, most of them are a result of clever wardrobe tricks. Look at your body in the mirror to identify your problem areas.

If the top part is decidedly larger than the bottom, then buy tops to minimize the upper area and always stay away from horizontal stripes.

If the bottom part of the body is heavy then wear necklines and colors that keep the eye upward. Discover your signature style and stick to it. A V-neckline top or dress is the best wardrobe weapon for a full-figure woman.

Hairstyle to suit your face

Some hairstyles make your face look thinner, while others make it look rounder. Hook yourself with a hairstyle that works to make your face seem thinner. For instance, if you have a round face then you should think about maintaining long hair.

Go for layered bangs that would help to slenderize your face. If you want a short hairstyle then you can go for a bob cut with razored ends. Apart from these, even highlights can help to create a vertical line on your face that makes your face look longer and slimmer.

Makeup Tricks

Makeup helps you to look slim instantly. One can create sculpted cheekbones or hide a double chin after understanding the high and low points of the face. Contouring and highlighting tricks can help you do the trick.

If you wish to downplay your double chin, then apply a darker color foundation on your jawline blending into the neck.

The illusion of depth will give your face a lot more definition and make it look slimmer. Also, always keep your eyebrows in shape.

Pose Perfect

Not only is it crucial to wear pantyhose under your clothes to hide the bulge, but also when you are in front of a camera learn to pose properly. Always turn sideways to the camera with one foot in front of the other.

Pull your head a little forward to ensure that the double chin disappears. Hold your arm away from the body, and gently suck your stomach in. If you cannot do all this, then just look away from the camera, turn suddenly towards it with a smile for a fresh look.

Stick to one color

This is a great fashion trick for all the plus-size women to take a lesson from. Take one single color and stick to it. This would create an elongating effect, which will make you look not only tall but slimmer as well.

Those who have a heavy midriff should stick away from wearing contrasting color uppers and lowers as this would draw unnecessary attention to the middle area.
Black is the best color for those who wish to hide their problem areas. An 'all black' outfit is vouched by many full-figured women to be their best wardrobe choice.
Well, if you don't want an 'all black' wardrobe then here is a trick for you to keep in mind: use bright colors to highlight your good features and darker ones to hide the bulges. Darker colors help to camouflage troubled areas of your body.

Heels your new BFF forever girl the right shoes, and she can conquer the world." - Marilyn Monroe.
Yes, girls! shoes can certainly do a lot for you.
Well, if you want to look taller and slimmer then you have to make heels your 'best friends forever.
Even the slightest heel can make your legs appear longer than they are. This is a fashion tip for a woman to vouch for. So, ditch your flats to elongate your body.

"

LIFE'S TOO SHORT
TO WEAR BORING
CLOTHES.

— CARLY CUSHNIE AND MICHELLE OCHS,
CUSHNIE ET OCHS —

Chapter 9

Dress Up As Per Your Body Type

Tags: A-line flared pants, A-line lehenga, A-line suit, Anarkali, angrakha style, apple body shape, belts, blouse waistline, boat neckline, bodycon dresses

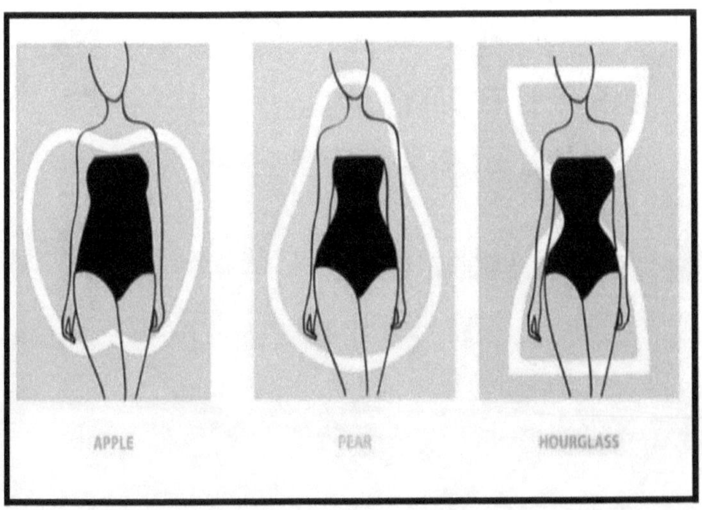

Dress Up As Per Your Body Type

Here we are gonna discuss the kind of clothing a woman should wear as per their body type more specifically with a plus-size woman.

One fashion rule doesn't apply to plus-size women, there are different types of plus-size which means different rules work for different body shapes. You may have the apple shape, pear shape, or an hourglass body type.

APPLE BODY TYPE

Her waist measurement is larger than your bust and hip area. This means you are bulkier in your waist and stomach area. Your legs will be comparatively toned and slimmer than your waist area. For this kind of body shape, the best silhouette is A-line.

You can wear A-line tops, dresses or kurtas. Everything A-line is perfect for you. A-line is narrower on top and flared on the bottom which will help to conceal your stomach and define your chest area.

In suits, you can wear flared suits like Anarkali or dresses like maxi dresses are good for you. Just keep one thing in mind that the waist fit of your dress is at your empire waistline. The basic motive of these dresses is to bring out the best feature of your body which in the case of an apple body shape is your empire waistline as this is the slimmest part of your body.

Similarly, peplum tops are best for you provided the waist of peplum falls on your empire waistline. Empire waist fit will not only make you taller but also slimmer.

In Indian wear, Angrakha and dresses, wrap-around dresses will work best for you as it also helps to define your waist. Don't wear suits or dresses that are heavily embroidered on your natural waist area. It will highlight the broadest part of your body. So prefer lightly embroidered neck and sleeve designs or you can wear dresses with borders on flares.

Don't wear necklines that hug around your neckline collars and high necks. If you wear such necklines, it will make your upper body appear broader. V and Round necklines are good for you. Avoid square necklines as it is structured and will make your bust look wider.

In bottoms, you can wear high waist skirts. This means the waist should clutch around your empire waist instead of the natural waistline. This rule applied to lehengas and skirts both.

In pants, avoid wearing fitted trousers with small hems. If you do so, it will highlight your slim legs creating a visible comparison between your heavier upper torso and slimmer lower torso making you look bulkier. So, wear straight pants or A-line flared pants.

Dress Length

If you are wearing tops or shrugs then they should fall on your hip bone or mid-thigh. You can also check the length by standing straight. The point of legs where e fingers of hand touches will be your ideal length for tops.

You can wear dresses of any length and even dresses with a side cut that will help you reveal your legs that are one of the best parts of your body.

For sleeve length, If you are comfortable with your biceps then fitted body you can wear sleeveless, or else you can wear any sleeve except the one that ends your bust line, it will make your upper torso look broader.

You can also wear belts, avoid thick belts as they won't be much visible on your body frame. Wear a broad belt in your empire waist. It will highlight your slimmest part. Also, it will look best with a poofy skirt.

Color blocking is also good for you. In this, you can get the center panel of your dress in any color but side panels should be in dark colors to create an illusion. Or you can reverse, dark inside and light outside.

You have a bulkier lower body and comparatively slimmer upper body. Your size for bottom wear is larger than your upper wear. For eg., You wear XL in pants and L for pants. A-Line dresses are best for you too. You can wear A-line kurtas, tops, or dresses as they will help to conceal your hips and thighs while defining your slimmer upper body.

You have to focus on highlighting your upper body. The more you highlight your upper short-fitted body the more balance you will create in your body proportion. You can wear tops or other upper wear in bright colors or with embroidery.

For Anarkali or Maxi Dresses, you have to wear dresses with empire waistlines similarly to apple body types. You can have embroidered or printed yoke attached to your Anarkali or gowns.

You can wear long kurtas with trousers or palazzos. Avoid short-fitted kurtas as they will define your hips and thighs. For adding an illusion of length, long kurtas are helpful. Instead of tightly fitted bottoms, wear palazzos.

Avoid fish cut or mermaid fit lehenga. Go for A-line or kalidar lehengas. A line is a perfect silhouette for you for both upper and bottom wear.

One tip for you, don't buy pants according to your waist measurement. Instead, buy them according to your hip measurement as this is the widest part of your lower body. You have to get your waist altered for a perfect fit.

You have a lot of options for necklines. You can wear broad necklines as they will create a balance between your upper and lower body. Broad round, boat, or square necklines are good for you.

You can wear sweetheart necks, collars, ruffled tops. Anything that can add an element to your upper body will help. Heavily embroidered, pleated, ruffled, frilled, gathered, or off shoulders. This is an advantage of your body type. You can wear stylish upper wear.

You can wear any bright, neon, or pastel colors for upper wear. Any of your favorite prints can be used for upper wear.

Go for large jewelry neckpieces

You can also wear large and broad neckpieces to highlight your upper torso. So if you love wearing jewelry and you are pear-shaped, then Waist fit is really important for you. So whatever you wear a top or a kurta make sure you have a waist dart in it as it will perfectly define your waist.

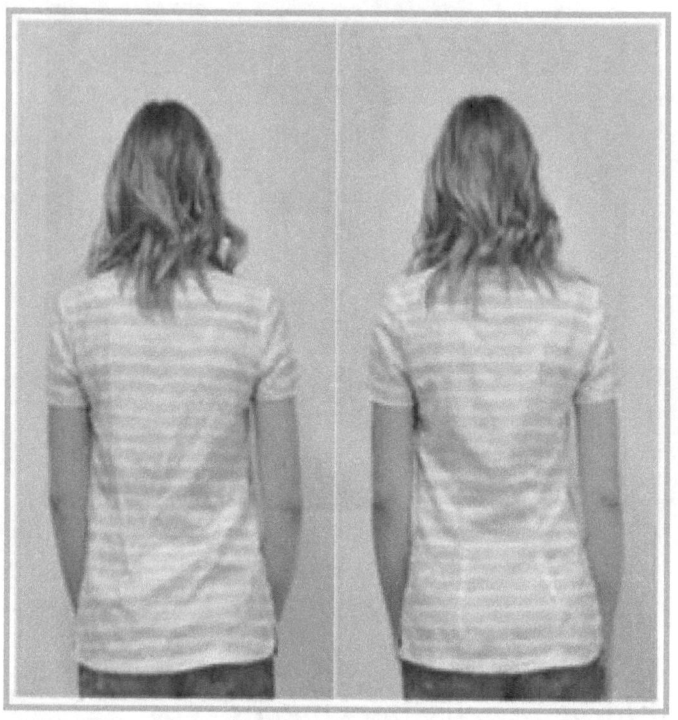

You can wear dark or neutral colors in bottoms. Avoid prints and if you like prints in the bottom then wear prints that are of the same color family and prints that are placed close to each other or dense prints.

HOURGLASS BODY SHAPE

If your waist size is less and your chest and hip size is more and measures almost the same then you have an hourglass body shape. You have a proper curvy body shape.

The basic dressing rule for your body is to flaunt it the way it is. Unlike the apple and pear body shapes where we focussed on the upper body for pears and the waist area for apples. You have to maintain your body shape as it is an hourglass body type.

Whatever style you wear, your bust and hip should be in proportion. Avoid wearing broad necklines as it will make your bust area appear larger than your bust which breaks the proportion. Round, scoop, and jewel necklines are good for you.

Unlike the other two body shapes, your dress yoke should be on your natural waist as that is your slimmest body part. Similarly, you should tie your lehenga or skirts on your natural waistline. Avoid wearing ruffled tops as they will hide your waist and break the bust and hip proportion. If you love such tops then wear them with poofy or flared skirts to balance your body shape. If you hide your shape then there is no point in being blessed with such a curvy body.

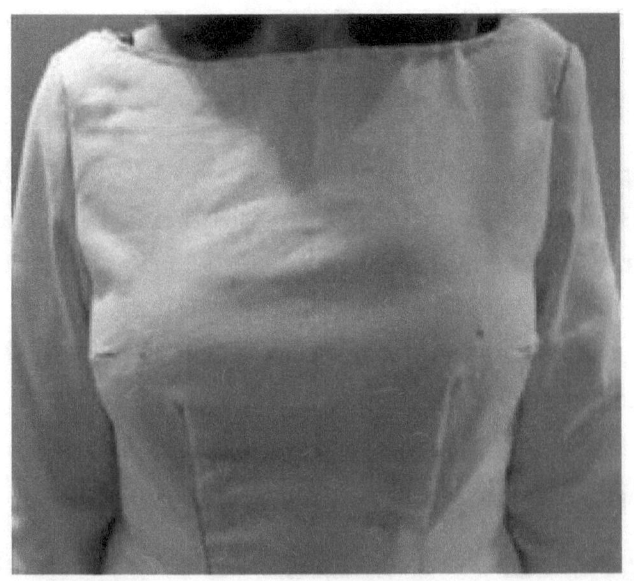

Waist Darts

These are important to you for a defined waistline. If you don't like waist darts in front of your dresses then at least have waist darts at the back of your top wear.

You can get embroidery done on your blouse waistline or your lehenga waist belt. You can wear broad belts with skirts or one-piece dresses.

Bodycon dresses are best for you to flaunt your curves. Whatever body shapes you are, flowy fabrics are good for you. You can wear silk, cotton, georgette, chiffon, and crepe. Avoid stiff fabric that gives boxy fits.

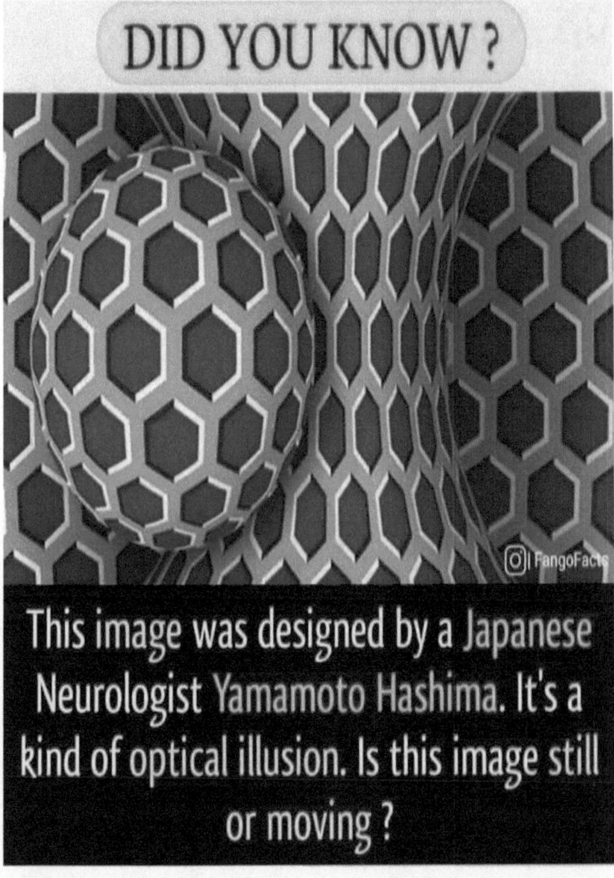

Chapter 10

Give Your Face An Angular Look With Makeup And Hair Style

Tags: eye makeup, facial features, facial look, hair styling, look book, fit body

Give Your Face An Angular Look With Makeup And Hair Style

With just a slight increase in weight, our face tends to look chubbier. The roundness is more profound. There are ways to make the face look a little less round. The two exclusive ways are: Face contours and Hairstyle. Let's know about these tips more closely.

Face Contour

Face contour is done by using different shades or blushers. Highlight the cheekbone with a light blush-on shade and then dab a little pinkish shade on the hollow of the sucked-in cheeks. Using a bronze shade on the cheekbone has a dramatic effect. The magic lies in the blending of the two shades. The face looks slightly tapered near the cheeks and chin.

Contouring can be done with creams or powders. Use fingertips to blend, if creams are used. In the case of powders use a brush to dab.

Hair Style

Allow your tresses to grow up to the shoulders. Allow a few strands to cover the sides of the face. This helps to cover the roundness of the face. Use darker hair color to darken the hairs near the scalp. This makes the face appear a little long.

The other way to create an 'angular' effect on the face would be to use fancy long earrings (danglers). These help to distract attention from the face. Allow a few locks to cover the portion near the scalp. This will break the circular shape of the forehead.

Tying a 'ponytail' also helps in giving the face an interesting angle. A long Ponytail helps to reduce the roundness of the face.

Eye Make-Up

Giving a feline feel to the eyes; makes them look classical. Extend the eyelashes with liners. Shape the eyebrows at an angle at the end of the usual circular one.

Trying a few techniques or combining a few variations will help you select an ideal way to make your face look thinner and graceful.

Phenomenal Woman

It's in the reach
of my arms,
the span of my hips,
the stride of my step,
the curl of my lips.
I'm a woman
phenomenally.
Phenomenal
Woman,
that's me.

Phenomenal Woman by Maya Angelou

Chapter 11

Top 6 Styling Tips To Hide Tummy Fat

Tags: High Waist Bottoms, Peplum Tops, A-Line Tops, Sarees/Anarkali Suits, A-Line Dresses, Tummy Tuckers

Top 6 Styling Tips To Hide Tummy Fat

Style Tip No.1 –

High Waist Bottoms:

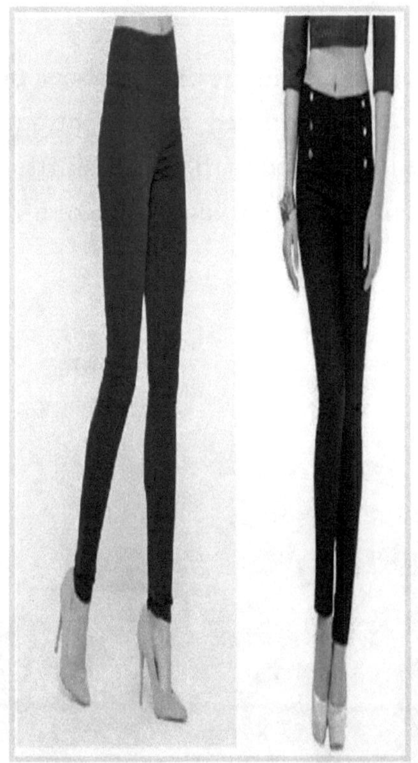

Say No to low waist jeans or bottoms. Instead, go for high waist jeans or jeggings. This will hide your tummy fat and side budges. This style of high waist jeans is in fashion these days which is good for curvy women like us.

Style Tip No. 2 –

Peplum Tops:

These types of tops are straight on the above area which gives a well-fitting look and are flared at the bottom that hides your tummy area. This looks good with sarees, skirts, or jeans. They are available everywhere in the markets online or offline.

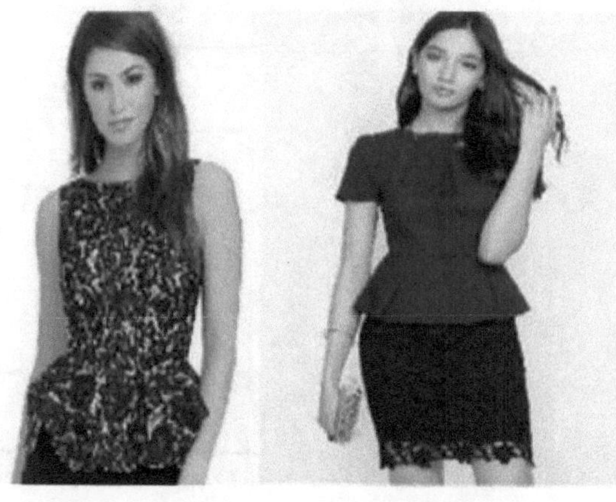

A-Line Tops:

It has a flair at the bottom. This fits comfortably toward the breast area and has a flair at the bottom which hides your tummy fat.

Style Tip No. 4 –

Sarees/Anarkali Suits:

With open pallu style, sarees give you a slimmer look. The Anarkali is well fitted to the breast area and has flared at the bottom that hides your tummy fat. Similarly, buy floor-length gowns to attend to any occasion and have a more stylish & trendy look.

Style Tip No. 5 –

A-Line High Waist Skirts:

Always wear A-Line Skirts above your waist area which can easily hide your tummy area instead of straight skirts that could reveal your bulgy tummy fat. Ethnic A-line Skirts with pleats, frills look more beautiful on curvy women especially.

Style Tip No. 6 –

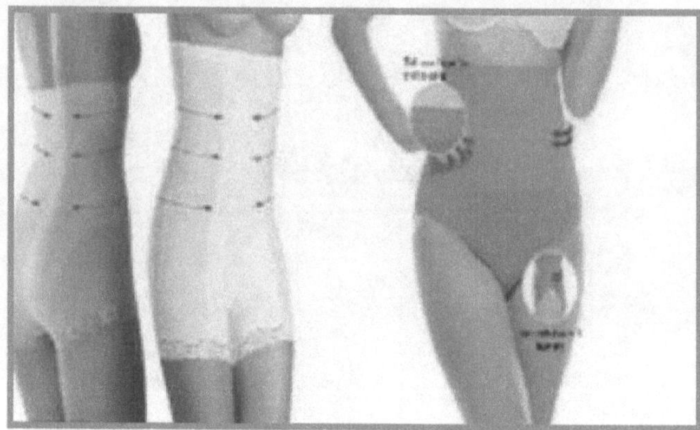

Tummy Tuckers:

To wear a well-fitted dress, you can wear tummy tuckers inside your dress. These body shapers are easily available in the market. You can use them especially on some special occasions like college farewells, parties, wedding functions or reception, etc. Never try it for regular use.

I'M NOT AN ARTIST. I'M A FASHION DESIGNER OF CLOTHES.
Manika Singla
Facebook @ethnoystmagz

Chapter 12

How To Mix and Match

Tags: body type, color combination, five rules, mix and match, plain with printed, same fabrics, work type

How To Mix and Match

We don't like to repeat dresses. Isn't it ?? Also, It's not possible to buy clothes at the time. Clothes can be repeated by mixing and matching different clothes so that new looks can be created with the same garment. So here we are giving you five rules to solve this general problem of girls like us !!

Rule 1: Colour Combination –

We can create different looks from basic wardrobe staples. The first rule is to pair in the same color combination. Some colors tch so perfectly such as black and white or black with red or color black with gold or beige, pink with green or pink with yellow or pink with white.

It's important to see what kind of color of work is done in the fabric for instance if there is an orange dupatta with golden work, then it will go with gold color kurta, it cannot be paired with a silver work suit, similarly, if there is a lehenga in different colors, then pair it with a dupatta of the matching color in lehenga

Rule 3: Pair Print with Plain –

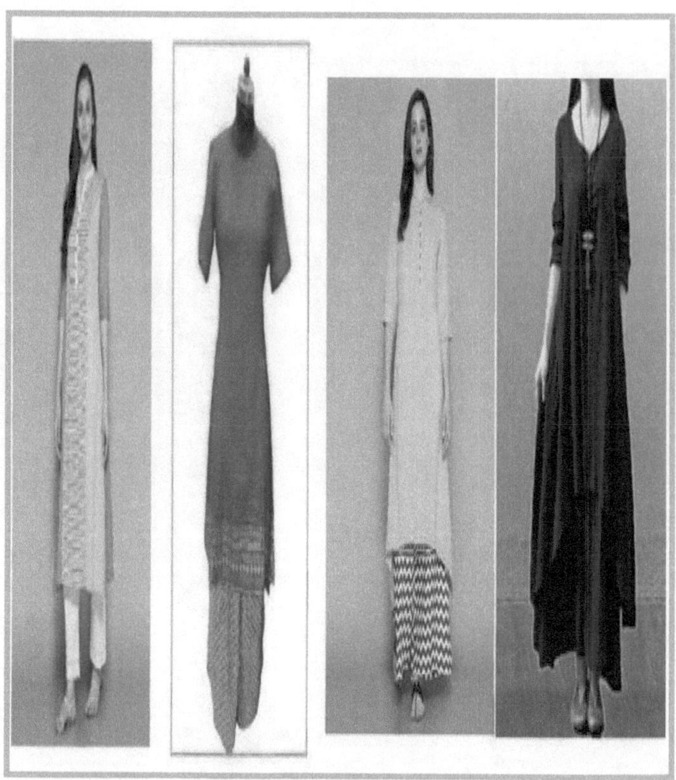

It looks much better if we pair a printed dupatta with a plain suit or printed skirt with a plain top. To make the clothing stand out, it always looks good to pair printed with plain fabric. However, It's not always true. Some people do that so flawlessly. Like a printed blazer with printed pants along with a plain top inside. But in general, if you do this, it will look much better.

Rule 4: Pair Same Fabrics –

Pair cotton kurta with cotton palazzo, silk suit with silk dupatta, synthetic top with the synthetic bottom. Otherwise, it will look too odd.

Rule 5: Dress According To Your Body –

For instance, if you have a tummy, then never go for crop tops, instead, go for long jackets. If you have heavy legs, then you could wear

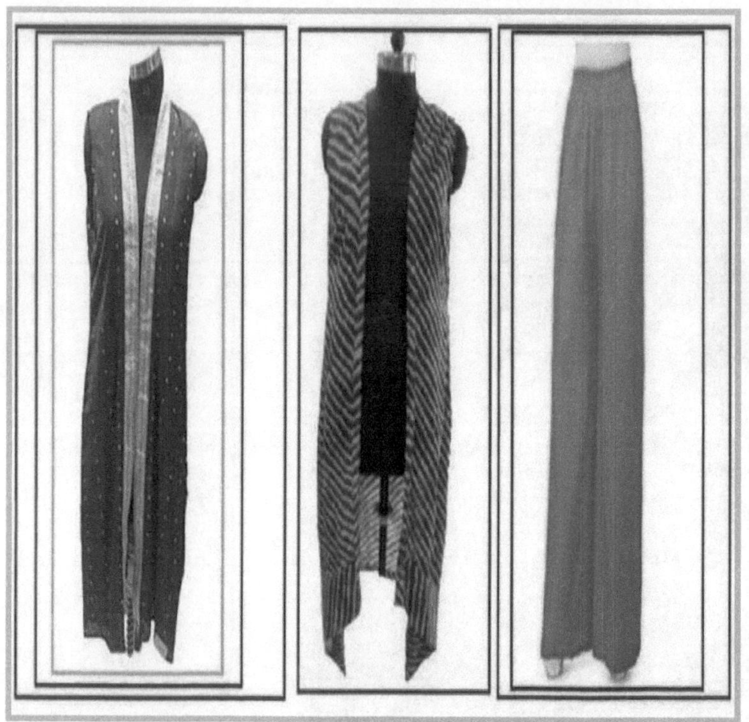

wider palazzos.

So, this is how to just mix and match and give a new look to your wardrobe. And nobody will come to know that you have repeated your clothes if you have followed these rules !!

DID YOU KNOW ?

Apples are more effective in waking
you up in the morning
than coffee

Eating cucumbers before
bed time can help you wake up
feeling refreshed and headache-free

Just 2 bananas will provide
you with enough energy
for an intense 90-minute workout.

3 carrots give you energy to walk
3 miles. They were first grown
as a medicine not food.

Chapter 13

Amazing Dress Alteration Ideas

Tags: alteration ideas, center panel insertion, Colour Blocking, criss cross knot on side panels, dress alterations, fabric   addition, fabric insertion, godet, godets, laces insertion

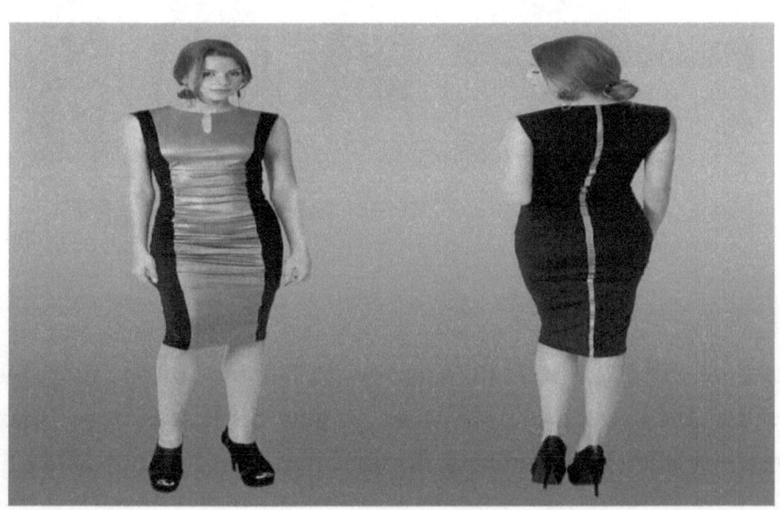

Amazing Dress Alteration Ideas

Here, we will talk about altering the clothes that you no more wear because they are too tight now. It may be kurtas, tops, maxis, dresses or even your trousers. So stay till the end of this article !!

The first and foremost commonly used method is to insert fabric in the side seams of your dress or kurta. Make sure the fabric you insert is cut uniformly. If you are inserting 2" wide fabric in front, then you need to insert 2" wide fabric in the back seam too. You have a lot of options in this, if you have plain kurta, then you can insert a plain panel or you can insert an opposite color panel too.

If you want to wear this kurta at a wedding or a party, then you can have laces placed on the side panel Insertion. There is one more benefit to this style. Many of you who ask for design ideas that can help your body frame appear slimmer, we told you about color blocking your outfits in our article "dress up as your body type". So this design will work like color blocking only. The side panel insertion will make your body frame appear narrower.

You can do the same thing with your trousers too. Insert a fabric panel in your trousers from waist to ankle. There are lots of options in this too.

You can have a colored panel or opposite color panel or the same color panel inserted. Or you can have laces placed on these side panels to make a trouser for your partywear suit.

Godet

It's a triangular piece of cloth that we can insert in tops, kurtas, skirts, or lehengas for adding an extra flare. This can be inserted after cutting a kurta from the center. You have to get the godet placed on both the backside of your kurta or top.

Here you can experiment with the godet fabric. You can use decorative fabrics, prints, or plain fabrics. Not only your old top will become of your size but also it will be designed into a new style.

Similarly, you can get center godets inserted in your pants too. You have to get them placed in your front and back sides of your pants. It will turn your straight pants into flared pants.

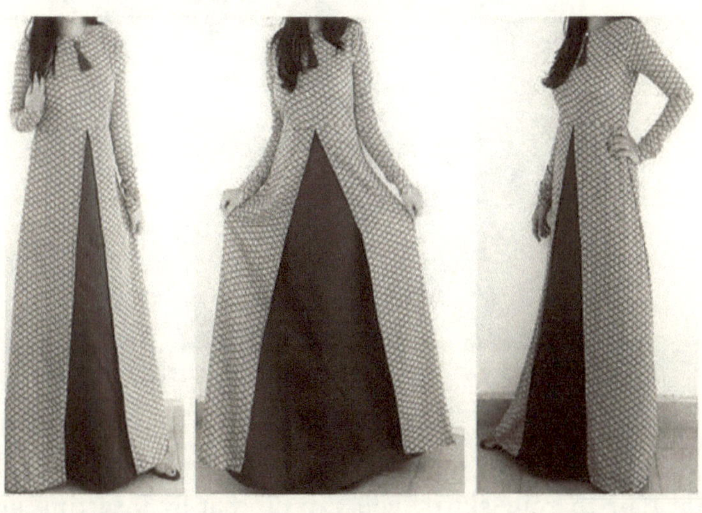

Next is placing a godet at the center-left of the dress. Again, you have a lot of fabric options here. You can use any kind of fabric plain or printed. In this, we have only changed the placement of the godet from center to center-left of your dress. You can add this to your A-line tops, kurtas, or maxis.

Multiple Godets

To add flair to your skirts, you can do that by inserting multiple godets after a few intervals like placing godets at a distance of 4"-6" from each other throughout your skirt. You can do this to add flair to your kurtas and tops too.

Side Seam Godets

You can get this inserted into the side seam of your dress, kurta, or top. Similarly, you can get a side seam godet inserted in your pants too. You have to get them placed inside the leg and outside the seam of your pants. It will turn your straight pants into flared top-wear pants.

Princess Line Inserts

Princess line insert is constructed for a better fit. So, the center has extra fabric added to the princess line. It will redesign your old kurta or top completely as your old top-wear will need everything to be constructed again except your neckline.

Center Panel Insertions

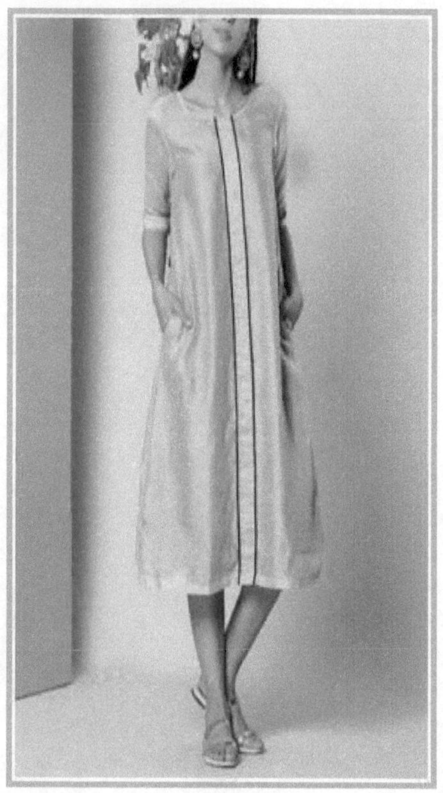

You can add a center panel to your kurtas and give them a jacket kind of look. Use it in your tops too for changing their style. But this will require more work as you have to get your necklines finished again. So, it needs extra effort but this design is really good.

It is good for your party-wear kurtas. This method will not only make your old kurtas fit you again but also the style will be changed into a jacket and also spending on remaking of these kurtas seems sensible as they are too expensive and need to be preserved for a long time. So spending a little more on them will not be an issue.

Spending on remaking your casual dresses by this method makes you feel like a wrong choice as this remaking may cost you more than the actual price of your casual kurta or top. So, it's a good option for heavy or party wear kurtas.

Criss Cross Knot on Side Panels

Next, this is a very interesting style that you can use to modify the very first style discussed which was inserting a side panel to your top wear. You can add loops and Doris in a criss-cross manner over the side panels. Also, add little poms or tassels at the end of Dori/string.

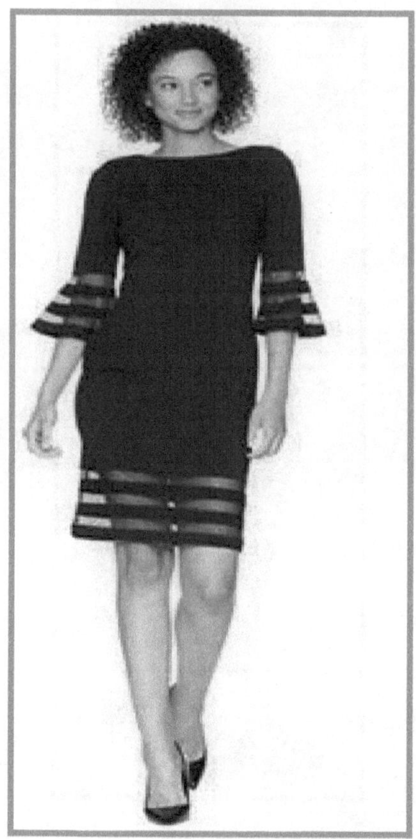

You can add net fabric to increase the length of your kurta or trouser. You need to insert extra fabric. It could be any fabric – plain, printed, embroidered, same color, or a different color. You can add piping or insertion lace at the joint.

To convert tops into A-line dresses, Add plain georgette to these tops and give a center-left slit. In this way, a pretty summer dress is ready for use.

You can wear it with trousers or palazzos. The best thing is it won't cost you much as you can use synthetic georgette for such a design.

"

Elegance is
the only beauty
that never fades.

— AUDREY HEPBURN —

Chapter 14

Top 10 Styling Hacks for Short Girls

Tags: A-line flowy Kurtis, heels, high bun hairstyle, high waisted bottoms, monotone patterns, narrow bottoms, Nude or pointed heels, photos from a low angle, short height, sling bag, or smaller handbags

Top 10 Styling Hacks For Short Girls

Here we discuss the top 10 styling hacks for short height women –

Style Tip No 1

Say yes to high-waisted bottoms as it gives an illusion for a taller frame. So you can go for tucked-in shirts with that or crop tops.

Style Tip No 2

If you want to wear wide palazzos, then wear heels with it because palazzos cover the heels and give a kin illusion of a taller frame. So wear wide palazzos with heels. If you are not a heels person then go for narrow bottoms like cigarette pants or straight pants. They look better than wide palazzos

Style Tip No 3

Wear A-line flowy kurtas than normal Kurtis which just cuts the frame and makes you look shorter. So wear A-line Kurtis which are continuously flowing from top to bottom.

Style Tip No 4

Wear V neckline tops rather than closed round tops as they will make you look taller. You can go for V neck Kurtis in ethnic wear or tops in westerns.

Style Tip No 5

Vertically striped pattern bottoms such as pants or culottes draw all your attention to legs that look larger in size that makes the whole frame longer

Style Tip No 6

Nude or pointed heels are best for you that match your skin tone as they will make you look longer and will also help you look taller.

Style Tip No 7

Wear solid combinations instead of prints like solid tops with solid bottoms rather than prints. Monotone patterns like black on black combination with black pants with black tops or black kurtas with black palazzos, pink kurta with pink palazzo. This solid on the solid combination and that too in the same color will make you look longer. So go for solids than prints.

Style Tip No 8

Wear a high bun hairstyle. It adds inches to the whole frame. So a high bun will help you look taller.

Style Tip No 9

Take photos not from the front but at a low angle. The more you take the picture from down, the taller your whole frame will look.

Style Tip No 10

Wear a thin waist belt as this will lengthen your legs and opt for a sling bag or smaller handbags instead of a gigantic shoulder bag. It doesn't work well in terms of proportion for someone who is a pity. So ditch the big-size bag !!

JUST BE
YOUR
OWN
UNIQUE
BEAUTIFUL
SELF

Chapter 15

25 Must-Follow Relationship Rules for Happy Love/Marriage

Tags: love, marriage, relationship, relationship rules, rules

25 Must-Follow Relationship Rules for Happy Love/Marriage

To many people, love is tricky and confusing. And to many others, love is just a mirage. They may be in a relationship and still never experience true love. But every new relationship has the potential to blossom into something spectacular and wonderful, just as long as you remember the relationship rules that matter the most.

Relationship rules for successful love

There are a few relationship rules that can change a drifting relationship into a romantic one. But as trivial and simple as they may seem, it's something that needs a lot of effort and dedication to achieve. Someone once said that falling in love should be effortless. True, falling in love is easy, but staying in love always needs a bit of work. Just as long as working in a relationship feels less like work and more like fun, you should be just fine.

25 relationship rules that matter

Follow these relationship rules in our relationship, irrespective of whether it's new or old. As long as you're committed to creating a better relationship, you'd have no trouble creating magical experiences out of love.

#1 Try your best to love your partner unconditionally even if it seems hard not to be selfish.

#2 Think from your partner's perspective when it comes to matters of the heart.

#3 End an argument as soon as possible, even if hugging your partner is the last thing on your mind.

#4 Make love regularly, but never allot times for it. Scheduling a time for sex makes it a chore that can start to become a bore.

#5 Communicate with each other and grow together in love, but never grow apart with lack of communication as the years pass by.

#6 Learn to give space to each other to become better individuals. Even the closest of relationships need some alone time to miss each other now and then.

#7 Never take each other for granted. This is the easiest way to fall prey to affairs and arguments.

#8 Say a white lie when you need to, especially if it's a little lie that won't change our relationship, but will make your partner feel happy.

#9 Never shy away from positive criticism. As long as you say it constructively, it'll help your partner become a better person.

#10 Be the shoulder to lean on, no matter what. Tough times are the most testing phases of a relationship. Stand by your partner, and when the storm ends, love will shine brighter.

#11 Never argue in public but indulge in the public display of affection.

#12 Date each other even if you've been together for years. It keeps the love alive.

#13 Look sexy for each other, and that includes a flat tummy. Just because you're in a relationship doesn't mean you should let yourself go and look shabby.

#14 Compliment your partner, even if it's a regular chore or habit. Compliments are the best way to thank a special someone for the effort they've taken for you, however small it may be.

#15 Celebrate the special days. Birthdays and anniversaries may repeat themselves too many times, but it's these milestones that create memories.

#16 Never intentionally try to make your partner feel bad. It'll leave a lasting scar that can hurt the relationship.

#17 Learn to forgive without holding grudges. As hard as it may be, forgiveness is one of the qualities of true love that matters most in a relationship.

#18 Respect your partner wholeheartedly.

#19 Understand that your partner can have crushes on others too. It's a difficult thought, but if you admire someone else, so can your partner.

#20 Trust your partner and your instincts, even if others say otherwise.

#21 Never grumble or badmouth each other even if you're tempted to, out of anger or frustration.

#22 Learn to spend quality time with each other. There's no better way to fall more in love with each other as the relationship grows.

#23 Behave like children now and then. A few pillow fights or cute wrestles can never hurt anyone. But it can help both of you enjoy the relationship.

#24 Be spontaneous with your affections. Don't always wait for special occasions or moments to express your love. Spontaneous surprises are always happier than planned surprises.

#25 Whatever works! No relationship is alike. Instead of learning from someone else's relationship, learn from your own relationship's successes and failures.

These relationship rules could seem simple, but following them to the tee can make all the difference between a romantic relationship and a failed affair. If you do treasure your love, make a difference with these tips. You won't regret it!

WHAT YOU CHOOSE TO FOCUS ON...
LOVE
WORRY
SELF-DOUBT
GUILT
ANXIETY
...WILL GROW

Chapter 16

Facts about being Overweight

Tags: BMI, obesity, overweight facts

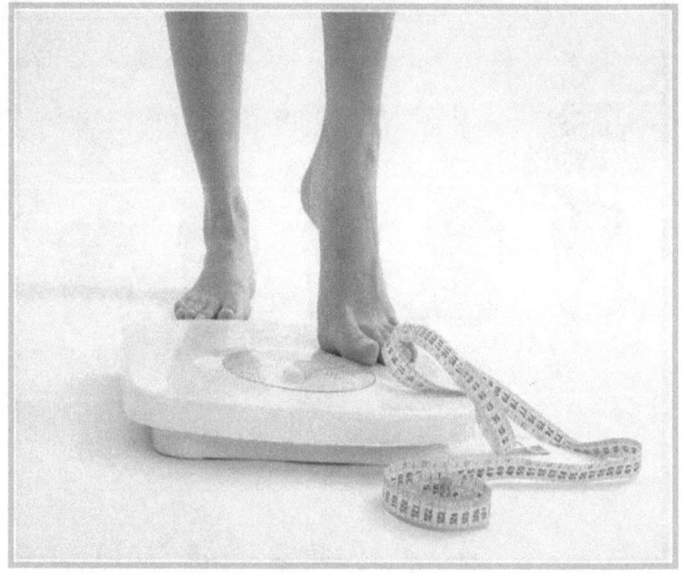

Facts about being Overweight

The fact is people are getting fatter and fatter. Obesity rates are on the rise and, in many countries, up to a third of the population are obese and over half are overweight. Whose fault is that?
The answer to this question should be simple: It's your fault. Because if you are fat, you eat too much and move too little! Simple really. However, before we can agree on this, let's just look at a few truths.
I don't want to be fat, and I can't imagine that there is anyone out there who does. Being overweight or obese makes so many aspects of our lives harder and is one of the major causes of global deaths.
It is undeniable that being fat is bad for our health and I would add that it often knocks our confidence; makes us less productive; less attractive and overall, less happy. So, if we had a choice, would anyone choose to be obese? I guess not.

Everyone understands the principles though: we gain weight when we eat more calories than we burn; we lose weight when we eat fewer calories than we burn; we stay the same weight when we eat the same calories we burn. An average man burns about 2,500 calories per day. For an average woman, this figure is around 2,000 calories.

We are obese if our body mass index is 30 or higher and we are overweight if our body mass index is 25 or higher. Our body mass index (BMI) puts our weight with our height using the formula below (or you can use any of the online BMI calculation websites).

BMI = (Weight in Kilograms / (Height in Meters x Height in Meters))

This means weight gain is caused by an imbalance of calories in' versus 'calories out'. But is this the whole truth? Yes, and no. Other factors play a role and are often forgotten in the discussion.

If we take a sample of people, and all of them eat the same and exercise the same, some will put on (or lose) more weight than others. It is a simple fact of life that for some people it is easier to lose weight and keep it off than for others.

For example, I know some yellow-greenAnandamideo eat a very unhealthy and fatty diet, never exercise, and still have a flatter stomach than me (Yes, that is annoying!). One reason for it is that we all have different metabolic rates; some store calories and consume them slowly; others burn them off quickly and efficiently.

Among our distant ancestors, people with slow metabolic rates were the winners because it kept them going for longer. It meant they could survive longer without finding food. Today, where food is available all of the time, slow metabolisms put us at a disadvantage because we gain weight more easily.

Another truth is that our body is programmed to seek out fatty and sugary foods because way back in time it was good for us. Fatty and sugary foods would give us the energy to fight and hunt successfully.

Unfortunately, evolution hasn't kept up with the pace of change. Today, we no longer need calories to overdose on fatty and sugary foods, but our brain still tells us to do so. Some people are more disciplined and have more self-control, which means they can stop themselves from falling for the temptations. Others haven't.

An additional truth is that food companies are often hiding the fact that their products are not good for us. Confusing labeling and the overselling of the 'goodness' in products can confuse consumers and trap us into buying and eating food that is described as 'reduced calorie' or 'high in fiber' – but is, in fact, full of fats or sugars.

We could all now dwell on the fact that this is so unfair, or we could just accept it. Some people will find it easier to stay at a healthy weight than others – in the same way, some people find it easier to do the math, sing well, or run fast.

So where does this leave us now?

For me, there are two main conclusions here:

1. We all need to accept that many people are struggling to stay 'thin'. For most of them, it is not a choice but a constant battle against 'things' like slow metabolisms; their inability to resist temptation, and the 'mass selling' of food by companies and restaurants.

2. However, in the end, there is this undeniable truth: If you eat more calories than you burn, then you will get fatter. The very simple message here is fewer excuses, fewer calories, more exercise! And yes, some will find this harder than others but this is just the way it is (This conclusion is as much for me, as for everyone else. I keep fighting against my slow metabolism and all the temptations – but I am not giving up!)

Accessories
ETHNOYST MAGAZINE
Mood Board
Apparels
www.ethnicoyster.com

Chapter 17

Rock the Party

Tags: party looks, party wear, style fashionably, western wear

Rock the Party

We solve your dreaded what to wear conundrum with these glam looks that will make you the talk of any evening.
The party season is already upon us. It's the perfect excuse to slip into those sparkly numbers, wear your killer heels, put on some stunning lip color, and dazzle the night away.

With the invites pouring in, your social calendar will be jam-packed for the next few days. Whether you head out for a dinner party or cocktail with your girlfriends or a glamorous date, here's how to be a head-turner. Pick up your inspiration from these foolproof looks and own the room at any party!

Channel a vintage luxe feel in a textured long skirt paired with a black satin blouse, slicked black hair, show-stopping jewelry, and a bold red pout.

Unleash your inner disco diva in big heels, a pair of sequin leggings, and a sexy top in a neutral hue. Keep the makeup subtle, add volume to your hair and be the life of your party you are attending.

Let's accept it – we can never have enough bling. Slip into an all gold dress, team it with black stockings, a chic box-clutch, and smokey eyes and you will be set for a glam night out.

YES
I'M
DIVORCED
NO
IT DOESN'T
DEFINE ME

Chapter 18

An Inspiring Story of Rashmi Jain

Tags: Rashmi Jain, Social Activist, Indian Talent, Inspiring Story, Mrs. Social Butterfly

How A Beauty Made The Portfolio Of Success With The Brain?

The above quote beautifully personifies the value and power of women in society. If women are given a chance and opportunity to pursue and achieve their dreams, then they can make anything in the world possible. Time and again, a lot of women have not only proved their worth but also inspired others to take charge of their lives.

One such revolutionary woman is Rashmi Jain, who, despite all odds, created a unique place by starting her career in modeling after 15 years of marriage. Her journey is beyond factors such as age, number, marital status, and color, and that is why it should be known to everyone.

"If you want something said, ask a man; if you want something done, ask a woman." - Margaret Thatcher

Haunted Childhood And Its Impact

Rashmi was born on February 25, 1983, in Allahabad, a city famous for its 'Triveni Sangam' and 'Kumbh Mela'. Everything was going smooth for her in the holy city until her family shifted to Delhi during her 3rd standard. She was doing her best in her studies till now in Allahabad, but suddenly her studies got impacted in Delhi as something in their new house started haunting her.

She found herself locked in the rooms and bathroom with all walls suddenly appearing to be filled with red blood. She tried justifying her terror to her mother, but that was of no use as her mother assumed all those incidents were part of a mere horrible dream. Her continuous efforts to make her parents understand the effects of those horrendous incidents were in vain, and she went to such a sad state that her teachers also started complaining about her behavior and low marks.

However, a similar incident jolted her mother's consciousness when she got locked in the bathroom and heard weird voices. This incident forced the whole family to shift to Ludhiana to get rid of the evil soul in the haunted house. This incident opened the eyes of her parents, and they started relying on finding the truth behind every concern raised by the children, which should be the case with each parent-child relationship of the world.

"Without darkness, nothing comes to birth, as without light nothing flowers" - May Sarton

After moving to Ludhiana, Rashmi successfully came out of her depression owing to her inner strengths and belief in herself. However, her path was still full of hurdles, and the most significant challenge she faced, along with her one sister and brother, was to get admission to a good school. Call it her bad luck or destiny, her family had shifted to Ludhiana when the session was started, and no school was ready to get them enrolled when more than half of the course was already being completed.

The problems never seemed to end when Rashmi had to learn a completely different language, Punjabi, in just ten days. As every school of Ludhiana conducts a compulsory test of the Punjabi language. It seems challenges were becoming part and parcel of her life, and a little girl was fighting with all of them with her full strength.

By god's grace, she finally got admission to a reputed school, and within one year of joining, she secured 5th rank in the overall result of her class and went on to become one of the best students the school had ever witnessed.

As time passed, Rashmi became more famous with the title of 'Miss Farewell', and impressed everyone so much that even the principal of the school wanted her as his daughter-in-law. She indeed became a charismatic figure with great appeal to the public, and her persona was of no match in the school.

Ups And Downs Of Life

"Be a girl with a mind, a woman with attitude, and a lady with class."
Life has its own rules, and sometimes they change before even getting noticed. The same happened with Rashmi, who got married at the age of 20 after she completed her BCA. However, she was married to a family of open-minded people who were very supportive in every step of her, including further studies. While enrolling herself in an MBA course to continue her education, she got the news of her pregnancy.

Her family assured their full support and asked her to focus on her studies along with giving birth to a baby. Sadly, she was only aware of the hurdles most of the women used to face after marriage and how it is considered as an end of their life in terms of freedom. But, surprisingly, it was a completely different journey for Rashmi as she was able to handle both her studies and family simultaneously, along with full support from everyone.

One of the incidents that displayed the real picture of family care was when she went for her final MBA exams in Chandigarh after months of giving birth to her daughter through the surgical process. And, her mother-in-law used to wait outside the exam center with the newborn baby till the exam got over. This type of bonding and love helped Rashmi to secure 97% marks in her MBA. Not only this, she went ahead and completed a digital marketing course to boost her career in the right direction.

Peaks And Valleys Of Modelling

After completing her MBA and digital marketing, she went on to work on some digital marketing projects along with helping her parents in managing their boutique. She was using all her talent and expertise in every possible manner, and one day decided to take the next step in her career after she came across an advertisement of Haut Monde, Mrs. India worldwide 2019. She was always keen to do something different, and this platform was the perfect answer to all her questions.

"Feminism isn't about making women stronger. Women are already strong, it's about changing the way the world perceives that strength." - G.D. Anderson

However, like previous times, many challenges were waiting for her, and the very first one was the lack of prior experience in professional modeling. One should be well prepared when aiming to participate in a show of such high esteem. She knew her abilities, and to enhance them further, she joined grooming classes. But the story did not end here as the biggest challenge of society disapproving her participation after 15 years of marriage started haunting her.

Most of the people started laughing at the news of her involvement, and others saw modeling nothing more than a glamorous world. But she was adamant to not give up on her dreams and followed a simple principle of 'Kuch Toh Log Kahenge'. It helps her to overcome any discouragement, and she keeps moving ahead on her path to achieving success.

Journey To Haut Monde

Through her continuous interaction with ladies and other socially active people, she got a clear overview of all the problems faced by women and society. Common Universal themes and issues became her key targets, and she was able to provide real insight about prevalent topics like Environment Degradation, Gender Inequality, Independence Day, and Menstrual cycle through her speeches and acts.

Soon, she became a famous social activist and was awarded special women empowering awards like 'Aaj Ki Naari', 'Smart Wonder women', and 'Pride of India'. It was the start of her journey, but her dream of bringing a change in the world was getting better day by day.

"We do not need magic to change the world, we carry all the power we need inside ourselves already: we have the power to imagine better." - J.K. Rowling

It is always good to have role models in your life, and Rashmi did choose the perfect ones for his life-changing journey. MAA Anandamida, a meditation facilitator and her mentor, taught her to love herself the first as people who don't love themselves, can't love others with their full potential.

The other role model is none other than the former Miss Universe Sushmita Sen, who is a real beauty from both inside and outside. Rashmi has always dreamed of living a life like her, which will be full of kindness and humanity. These two became her soul and helped her to follow a path where she can lead from the front for anyone who is looking for inspiration in life.

"A role model can teach you to love and respect yourself" - Tionne Watkins
Whenever there was any low point during her preparation, then she used to focus on her goal of changing the perception of the world about modeling. It was her dream to become an inspiration for all silent women who are unable to follow her dreams due to gender inequality and discrimination at every point in this dark society.

At the Haut Monde event, she became the voice and roar of all those women and spoke about the social issues and programs in front of millions of people. Her performance in the show not only made her a finalist of this great event but also helped him to win the title of 'Mrs. Social Butterfly'.

This title signifies a beautiful woman flying across society to break the discriminated laws of society and bring a new world full of colors. She set herself to be a leader who wants to inspire others by leading from the front to make this world a better place to live through strong determination.

After Effects Of Success

"Women speaking up for themselves, and for those around them is the strongest force we have to change the world." - Melinda Gates

The best part of her journey throughout the Haut Monde event was the experience and motivation she got to continue her work in the social space. She also got some great friends on her journey, which are now an integral part of her life.

Her life completely changed after the event, and she realized the same when everyone started giving importance to her because of the T-shirt of Haut Monde she was wearing. She feels like a celebrity, and of course, she deserves that after doing so much hard work to follow her passion.

Not only this, many people who were opposing her participation earlier became her fan, and she was invited as the Guest of Honor in many modeling, dancing, and singing shows. Although it was not possible to change the whole society with one event, she certainly made many people appreciate her talent and power as a woman in the world.

Conclusion

"Setting an example is not the main means of influencing another, it is the only means." - Albert Einstein

Rashmi did not choose this profession only for herself, but her most significant motive was to educate people about the truth of modeling, which is not only limited to the glamour world. She has been trying to reach a higher number of people on public and social platforms so that social themes and issues can get their fair share of discussions.

Her success in modeling has paved the way for all aspiring models who want to gather knowledge and experience while building their self-confidence. She believes in the overall growth of India, and this can only be achieved when there is no discrimination based on gender, color, and even married or unmarried.

"You need to learn to say no and need to recognize when you're being exploited. You will get your due, according to your talent"
Radhika Apte
ETHNOYST MAGAZINE
www.ethnicoyster.com

Chapter 19

Poetry by Butch Decatoria - "I Am She"

Tags: Meaning, Poem

I Am She" by Butch Decatoria

This poem talks about the roles of a woman and how she loves through each role. The poet describes herself as the one who suffers the most to bring a new life into this world, and is, therefore, the one who will stay awake at night worrying over her child. The poet says she's equal in strength and ready to charge into the war by "his" side.

I am she
Who compliments & completes
The dream-lover and wishes
Made when he is asleep.
I am she
Who suffers the most,
Giving birth, cradling ghosts,
As the crone or maid,
(Once and always)

Sister, mother, daughter, wife.
I am she
Who waits through the night.
I am she
Who equals the strength?
Of his light.

"See me with your loving eyes,
See me more than the tears I've cried!"
I am she
Who is willing
To go with him to war,
Not a man but as an equal,
(I'm both soft yet hard)
I am she
To whom he'll give his heart
I am the tunnel's bright end
I am where
The family starts,
The breast which nurses small men.

I am she
The twin,
The Juliet,
The Goddess divine!
I am she

Who deserves the same
in life, and for all time.
(Peace is...)
I am she

I am you
I am her
I am the one beside
And inside
She is I...
The romance in the dress,
Patient Partner to the ends,
Tiny dancer on the floor
I am
The one that loves you
Forever &
Evermore.

STYLE
IS VERY PERSONAL

It has nothing to do with fashion.
Fashion is over quickly.
STYLE IS FOREVER

– RALPH LAUREN

Chapter 20

Fashion Glossary

Tags: Fashion Terms, Meanings

Fashion Glossary

Accent
Emphasis is given to a distinctive characteristic of a garment like color or trimming or accessory.

a la mode
The French term for fashion.

Androgynous
Androgyny refers to a look that is of indeterminate gender. Most commonly this look features garments and style traits that are commonly associated with the opposite gender to the wearer. i.e. women wearing ties, brogues, and oversized dress shirts.

Applique
Applique is a method of decorating garments in which one fabric is applied to another, often with floral and leaf patterns, but can be of any design and are stitched around the edges.

Accent shades

Bright dark colors like fluorescent colors. These are used as an emphasis rather than as the whole color of a design.

Art deco
Style incorporating geometric patterns in typical colors of yellow green gold silver and black.

Art Nouveau
A style that incorporates linear and curvilinear designs.

Anime
Anime is short for animation and refers to a dressing style that follows the fashion of Japanese Anime cartoons. Mostly features punk-style clothing.

Anti Fashion
Dressing in styles different from the fashion of the day; showing indifference to fashion and its varying trends.

Antique style
A style of the past.

Anti Pill
Treatment is done on fabric to increase the wear resistance, preventing the uneven and worn look of the fabric surface.

Achromatic colors
This refers to having no color; in fashion, it means black or white colors.

Accouterments
A popular or the latest style of clothing, hair, decoration, or behavior.

Avant-Garde
Refers to never seen before innovative designs by designers who are original thinkers bringing change to fashion.

Beaumonde
The fashionable world.

Bespoke
This refers to a made-to-order garment made as per the customer's characteristic measurements and specifications. Usually said about men's formal clothes or wedding clothes

Chemise
A loose-fitting dress that hangs straight from the shoulders without a defined waist

Capsule wardrobe
This is a term used for a collection of a few timeless and essential items of clothing.

Cosmopolitan
A dress style that is universal rather than localized.

Clique
As per Wikipedia clique is a small close-knit group of people who do not readily allow others to join them. In fashion, clique refers to a group of very fashion-conscious people who share a common sense of style.

Collection
A set of creations of a designer for a particular season.

Color blocking
This is a technique in which large blocks of solid-colored fabric are joined (usually sewn) to form the garment; placing blocks of different colors side by side this way provides a visually striking effect.

Camouflage clothing

Design with elements of camouflage in it like the print/khaki color.

Composite style
A combination of distinct styles; simple and refined; cool and feminine; feminine and flirtatious; funky and fun.

Costume jewelry
This is jewelry made to complement a particular fashionable garment/collection; usually inexpensive than real jewelry.

Darts
A sewn-in fold designed to give garments shape. In particular around the bust, waist, and hip areas.

Design elements
In fashion, this refers to Color, Shape, line, texture, balance, harmony, proportion, pattern, etc which are very important in designing well-liked clothes.

Diffusion Line

A modestly priced line of garments made by an haute couture designer.

Embellishments
A superfluous ornament that adds beauty or elegance.

Exotic
A style that is fascinating and evoking the look of a foreign land.

The eclectic style of fashion
This is a fashion style composed of elements drawn from various sources; A mix of various styles.

Empire Line
Low cut dress with a high waistline and short bodice.

Fad
A fashion that becomes popular in a culture or subcultures relatively quickly, remains popular, often for a rather brief period, then loses popularity dramatically

Fit and Flare
This refers to a dress style characterized by a form-fitting Bodice with a skirt that flares out towards the hemline, often with pleats or folds.

Gingham
A lightweight cotton cloth, usually checked. Typically combines white with red, blue, or green.

Glam
Music-related fashion from the early and mid-1970s with colorful ambisexual outfits, such as platform shoes and single piece glitter suits.

Gradation
Shades of the same color.

Haute Couture
Exclusive custom-fitted fashions are the pinnacle of the fashion industry. French for high sewing or dressmaking.

Hem
The edge of a piece of cloth or garment is folded up and sewn down to enclose the cut edge so that it cannot unravel.

Hounds-tooth
A duotone textile pattern of checks and four-pointed shapes, used particularly for outerwear, jackets, and skirts.

Inseam

The seam in a trouser/pants or short that runs from the crotch to the hem. Leg length is measured based on the inseam. Most often refers to the inside seam of pants. It also refers to the measurement from the pant crotch down to where the pant leg falls on the shoe; the inner seam on the legs of a pair of pants.

Jacquard Weaving

A versatile weaving method that allows a warp thread to be raised independently of the other wrapping threads.

Kilt

A one-piece garment from Scotland made from tartan or plaid cloth.

Kitsch

In fashion refers to low-quality style; garish style

Knock Off

A design that is a copy of a more expensive clothing

Knife–pleat

Very narrow pleats pressed to form regular sharp pleats to skirts and dresses. Particularly popular from the 1920s to the 1950s.

Lame

Shiny fabric made with either gold or silver metallic threads. Luxurious and glamorous.

Lapel

The two triangular pieces of cloth that extend from the collar of a suit jacket

Look Book
A publication featuring styles and conceptual creative ideas, influences, and inspirations.

Macrame
Knotting technique popular in home furnishings. Became associated with clothing in the 1960s and has had subsequent rebirths since the 1990s mainly in the form of handbags.

Monochromatic
The use of a single color.

Melange
A fashion is a mixture, combination of things, elements, or trends

Minimalist
A simple understated look; a fashion consisting of simple styles and plain colors.

Monotone clothing
Clothes of a single color

Mood Board
A physical or digital collage of design ideas used by fashion designers to consolidate their collections or get ideas. Will have details of an idea, drawings or photos, fabric swatches, etc.

Motif
A design used in a pattern/print/embroidery etc; usually found recurring

Natural Fibres
Fibers from plants and animals that can be spun into thread such as wool, silk, linen, cotton, and hemp.

Neutral Colours

Neutral means without color. In fashion Classic colors like black, white, gray, brown colors beige, and sometimes blue is called neutral colors.

Neoprene
A man-made fabric, used for wetsuits and other water sports attire. Has a stiff, body-hugging quality that seals body heat in

Opaque
Non-transparent or sheer.

Ombre
This refers to the style in which color graduates from light to dark.

Peek-a-boo
Any part of a garment that has been cut-out to reveal skin or underwear.

Pret-a-Porter
Designer clothes sold in standard sizes rather than made to measure.

Panache
A style that represents flamboyance or confidence.

Pantone colors
Pantone colors refer to a color reference system developed by the company Pantone Inc that standardizes the colors in the CMYK process. The Pantone colors correspond exactly to the inks and dyes used to color the fabric by various industries, basically for printing purposes and manufacture of colored fabric.

Quilted
Padding technique enclosing a layer of wadding between two pieces of fabric, held in place by sewing a diamond pattern over fabrics

Ruche/Ruched(pronounced roosh)
Fabric gathered and sewn into a seam shorter than the length of the fabric. Often used for trim but also used to create draping and texture within the body of the garment

Seam
The join line formed when two pieces of fabric are sewn together

Sheer
A semi-transparent and flimsy fabric with a very fine knit, often used to produce tights, leggings, and stockings in addition to lingerie and blouses.

Silhouette
The outline or contour that a garment creates when worn.

Sartorial
Anything related to Tailoring, clothes, fashion, or style of dress.; Of or of tailors and their trade, it is also used with the quality of a dress

Tea-length
A dress or gown that extends to the end of the shin.

Theme board (mood board)
A board with fashion drawings, sketches, swatches are used to create a mood about a product.

Tulle
A very fine mesh-like net fabric, used in evening wear and bridal gowns.
Tunic
A long or short, usually sleeveless, straight, tubular garment.

Utilitarian

Clothing that primarily serves a functional purpose, such as providing warmth, protection, or some other practical use.

Variegated
A fabric produced with different colored yarns or threads to provide streaks, marks, or patches of different colors.

Vent
An opening in the fabric that allows for greater movement.

Vintage
Garments originating in, or whose design is inspired by, a previous era.

Weave
The pattern of interlinking threads or yarns called the warp and weft created during the cloth production process on a loom.

Yarn
Any long, continuous piece of entwined fiber that is used for the production of textiles or knits.

Yoke
A fabric cut that is seamed across the top of a shirt, trouser, or skirt.

Zeitgeist
The moral and intellectual trends of a given era. Taken from the German Zeit meaning time and geist meaning spirit, the term's literal translation is 'the spirit of the age'.

Don't Wait for someone
to bring flowers .
Plant your own gardern
and decorate your own soul .
Ethnoyst Magazine

About the Book

An inspirational yet practical guide to clothes shopping, discovering and developing a strong sense of personal style for fashion lovers!

In the book, the author distills her secrets into a fun, comprehensive style guide focused on rethinking your wardrobe like a fashion expert and making what's in your closet work for you. She provides real-world advice about everything style-related, including:

- Styling every garment you own in the best way
- Mastering the closet organization
- Which alterations are worth it
- Shopping thrift and vintage like a rockstar

Instead of repeating boring style rules, the author tells us to break the rules and get real about everything from apparel to accessories to showcase inevitable fashion statements. The book has lots of insider tips from the author's arsenal of hacks and expertise.

About the Author

Dr. Manika Singla

A Writer, Designer N Management Expert

The author has been a management expert, fashion designer, and writer. She is currently running a design studio named Ethnic Oyster from last 2014. Apart from this, she runs her online profiles on all major social media platforms (Facebook, Instagram, and youtube) by the name of 'ethnoystmagz' and 'ethnicoyster'

Before this fashion writing and successfully running this clothing venture, she worked as a professor and researcher in the management domain for many years. Several research papers, books, and articles in diverse domains of management, tourism, and fashion are published for known national, international journals and related sites.

Flair for writing, passion for designing the fabrics as well as self-learning about the technical aspects of the digital world had encouraged her to enter into this stream. Utilizing her previous skills of writing as a blogger and learning by doing through exhibitions & networking gives her the direction to move ahead progressively.

CLOTHES AREN'T GOING TO
CHANGE THE WORLD

*the women who
wear them will*

- ANNA KLEIN

Acknowledgment

Thank You, Readers!

This is the first edition of Ethnoyst Magazine.

This magazine is for you and by you. The mission is to educate female fashion lovers by sharing fashion know-how, styling hacks, beauty tricks, health/lifestyle tips, home decor DIY ideas, real-life stories, and relationship issues.
If you want to contribute in any manner (articles/ideas/photos/poems/stories, etc)
Please write to us at **ethnoysmagz@gmail.com**
(Subject to approval)

We would love to hear from you!

Ethnoyst Magazine | www.ethnicoyster.com